Brilliant Bob is Strong

Written by
Kenneth T Jolivet

Copyright © 2021 by Kenneth T Jolivet

ISBN: 978-1-7365139-2-7

Edited by Melissa Peitsch

Illustrated by Renata Christine

Book Layout by Solaja Slobodan

All rights reserved

It was a warm spring morning.

Brilliant Bob was getting ready for soccer practice.

In England and many other countries they call it football.

Bob ate a healthy breakfast that would give him energy to play.

He also made sure he warmed up by stretching all his muscles.

Brilliant Bob knew he needed to be strong for himself and his team.

A short time later, Brilliant Bob jumped into the van with his dad.

He was excited because they were picking up his best friends:

Dazzling Dave, Genuine George, and Superboy Sam.

They pretty much did everything together and they were all on the same soccer team.

But they each played different positions.

Brilliant Bob played
'Center Forward Striker.'

He loved the fast pace, strength and power he needed to get the ball into the goal from this position.

He liked to see the ball go into the net: the faster the better.

Brilliant Bob was fast,
strong and clever.

He could break away from the other kids, kick the ball on the move and make
the ball curve around the goalkeeper to score the goal.

Sometimes it looked like
slow motion magic.

Genuine George was also a striker, but he played 'Behind the Striker.'

He was very fast and could defend and strike, moving back and forth as needed.

Genuine George loved to run with bursts of speed, surprising the other boys he left behind.

Everyone who knew him called him the 'Cheetah' because he was so very fast.

The boys on the other teams couldn't keep up with Genuine George.

Dazzling Dave played 'Central Midfield.'

He wasn't quite as fast as Genuine George, but he could run fast and for a very long time without getting tired.

He was also creative and good at communicating with his team.

Dave loved to move the ball around, looking for openings to get the ball past the other boys.

And he did it often.

He could fool the other side, feigning moves to pass the ball so Brilliant Bob and Genuine George could shoot for the goal.

And Superboy Sam was given the very important job of goalkeeper.

It was his job to stop the ball from going into the net.

He played this position because he had lightning fast reflexes, and he could kick and throw the ball very far.

It was almost as if Superboy Sam could predict where the ball would be, fly through the air with ease, and catch or deflect the ball to stop it from going into the net.

It was very rare for anyone to get the ball past Superboy Sam.

Brilliant Bob, Dazzling Dave, Genuine George, and Superboy Sam practiced long and hard on this particular morning.

They were getting ready for the championship game that was only a week away.

The coach had some fantastic ideas, but they would take lots of practice to perfect.

This meant they needed to work extra hard at staying healthy and strong, practicing regularly, eating healthy food, and getting enough sleep.

Brilliant Bob, Dazzling Dave, Genuine George, and Superboy Sam knew they had to be strong if they were going to play their best and win.

So they each ate a balanced and healthy diet.

It was the first thing on their list of things to do.

Even if they sometimes didn't really like the healthy food their parents offered, they knew it was good for them and ate it anyway.

They learned that each type of food gave their body a different benefit.

That it was important to eat a balanced diet, not eating too much or too little of any one thing.

They learned that meat and beans had protein to help them build muscles.

So they ate different kinds of meat like steak, chicken, and fish.

They also learned to try different kinds of beans, chickpeas, and lentils because they were also packed with proteins.

And they tasted great.

The boys also learned about carbohydrates.

They learned these types of foods gave them energy and made them feel full.

Brilliant Bob loved potatoes of every kind and style.

Dazzling Dave loved bread, and any kind of sandwich, especially with a big juicy apple.

Genuine George loved corn and rice.

And Superboy Sam loved spaghetti and pasta of any shape.

All four boys loved bananas because they tasted great and were easy and quick to eat, especially at break time during practice.

The boys also knew that vegetables were very important because they were full of so many nutrients and vitamins their bodies needed.

The more colors the better.

Vegetables helped Brilliant Bob to be strong and powerful;

And Genuine George to be super fast like a cheetah;

And Dazzling Dave to be able to run all day without getting tired;

And Superboy Sam to react quickly, jump high, and nearly fly through the air to stop the ball.

That's why the boys did their best to eat two or three different vegetables with each meal.

Or a big, mixed salad.

Brilliant Bob, Dazzling Dave, Genuine George, and Superboy Sam made a promise to themselves and each other to be strong.

That's why they also pledged to each other that they would go to bed early and not mess around at bedtime.

Brilliant Bob, like most kids, had been a naughty boy in the past, reading his comic books at bedtime, in the dark with a flashlight.

Not any more!

The boys had learned that rest was important for being healthy and strong.

Which helped them to succeed and win games.

And they desperately wanted to win the championship.

So Brilliant Bob, Dazzling Dave, Genuine George, and Superboy Sam practiced every day after school.

They knew that you had to practice a lot to be good at what you do, and also to get and be strong.

That's why the four boys swore an oath to practice everyday at home after their homework was done.

They were going to win the championship title.

'Hi Five,' guys!

Before they knew it, those seven days had passed.

Today was the big game!

Brilliant Bob, Dazzling Dave, Genuine George, and Superboy Sam were ready.

They were going to play the team that won last year's championship.

That team had never lost a game.

Perhaps things were about to change?

It was a tough game.
Each team had a strong defense
and an even stronger offense.
Both teams displayed amazing
teamwork and athletic skills.
This is why the score was pretty
much tied for most of the match.
The first half was pegged at 1 to 1.
The second half was now 2 to 2,
with little time remaining.
Dazzling Dave had done a fantastic job of getting
the ball to Genuine George and Brilliant Bob.
Each had scored one goal.
And Superboy Sam had stopped five
goals from being scored.
The crowd could not believe it.
The tension was high.

Something needed
to be done and fast.

Zip, zag, zip...

With only a minute before the game
was over, Dazzling Dave slipped
by two boys and kicked the ball
thirty yards to Brilliant Bob.

It was a high and long pass.

Brilliant Bob chest-stopped it, quickly turned his body, and hip-twisted a powerful twenty-yard kick straight past the goalkeeper and into the net.

GOAL...

It was never even close.

There was just no time to react.

It was such a strong, powerful kick.

Brilliant Bob's strength was too much for the goalkeeper.

The score was now 3 to 2, with 10 seconds left, plus two extra minutes of additional time.

There was a mad scramble to do something.

The other side passed the ball from player to player many times, hoping for a break or hole.

But there was not enough time for the other side to score.

The defense was just too good.

The whistle blew. The game was over.

The four friends and their team were the new soccer champions!

All the practice;

The days of strength training;

The many nights of good rest and early, fresh starts;

And so many delicious and nutritious meals to feed their bodies: it all paid off.

Brilliant Bob, Dazzling Dave, Genuine George, and Superboy Sam learned that all these things make for strong boys.

That strength is important as strong young boys grow into strong men.

Brilliant Bob saw the strength of firemen, policemen and military men.

He saw that the men working in construction, roadwork, and farming were all very strong.

And he saw the strength in his favorite male athletes.

And Brilliant Bob saw how his dad worked out in the gym to get strong.

His dad was able to use his strength around the house.

Cutting big bushes, gardening, washing and waxing the cars, lifting heavy objects, shopping, and chopping firewood.

And he felt how strong his dad was when they wrestled and played games together.

Bob knew that one day he'd be as strong as his dad if he ate healthy, rested, and trained hard.

Brilliant Bob, Dazzling Dave, Genuine George and Superboy Sam had learned that being strong could help them;

To feel great;

To be a great athlete;

To be a great worker;

And to one day be a great husband and father!

In every way, it brought success, pride, and confidence.

Brilliant Bob made a promise to himself, and his friends, to always stay strong.

Being strong is cool!

Brilliant Bob thanks you for reading this book.
He also invites you to join him in his other great adventures where:

Brilliant Bob is Competitive
Brilliant Bob is Brave
Brilliant Bob is Curious
Brilliant Bob Takes a Risk
Brilliant Bob is Stoic
Brilliant Bob is Persistent

HIGH FIVE DUDE!

You can buy all seven books on Amazon.
And don't forget to visit Brilliant Bob's website at...

www.BrilliantBobKidBooks.com

CPSIA information can be obtained
at www.ICGtesting.com
Printed in the USA
LVHW071657030321
679611LV00025BA/949